How to be a Woman

Science of Living Series

M. Usman

Mendon Cottage Books

JD-Biz Publishing

Download Free Books!
http://MendonCottageBooks.com

Our books are available at

1. Amazon.com
2. Barnes and Noble
3. Itunes
4. Kobo
5. Smashwords
6. Google Play Books

Table of Contents

Preface

I want to thank and congratulate you for downloading the book, "How to be a Woman."

This eBook is an authentic guide that will help you as a woman to take on the challenges of life and learn the best way to live your life by maintaining great health, vigor, and also how to establish the life that you want to have. The book is appropriate for women, especially those who are in their prime, and it has all the information a woman needs to grow and develop in all aspects of your life.

Sometimes as a woman, you might experience so many challenges and transformations that some may end up weighing you down. If you are in such a predicament, this is just the right book for you. It'll help you grow mentally and you'll also have an intimate understanding of how life works out. you'll also understand why some things are happening in your life. Every woman deserves to have the best of what life has to offer, women need to be pleased and not miserable. By reading this book you will discover the areas in your life where you need to make changes in order to cultivate the kind of life that you desire.

As a woman, there are so many hardships you are bound to experience and endure; you are therefore required to know how best you can overcome certain issues. Every chapter of this book contains very useful information that you can use in order to maintain a dynamic lifestyle and make the best out of life. The author encourages you therefore to take your time to understand all that has been written in this special eBook for its life changing information.

Getting the Life You Want as a Woman

Women are often said to be very ambitious, as a woman you always want to lead a life aimed at ensuring you have the best of everything that life has to offer be it lifestyle or a mate/lover etc. This is quite an admirable trait that women usually have, and it is something their counterparts are usually keen to identify. Whenever a woman has attained any age between 40 up to 65 years old, the whole world usually tends to open up to her. Another fact to take into account is that there are so many transformations and challenges that she will be experiencing during this period. These changes could range from increased parental/spouse responsibilities, encountering break downs and also physical transformations, something that is quite inevitable. And as a woman you always have your dreams and desire that you aspire to realize in your lifetime. It is not an abnormal thing as a woman to want to be conspicuous from others. This need always gives a woman the stimulus to understand who she really is and most importantly how she can strategize on the best ways to create the life that she wants.

On your journey to make the best out of what life has to offer, it really helps to identify and know the things that actually define you, what you feel about the current state of your life and what you need to do in order to build up a life that is more accomplished and rewarding. Such kind of life usually goes beyond the boundaries of success, wealth, riches, or even happiness. If you really want to live a happy life then there are so many things that you need to put in to perspective such as fitness, health, your living standard, just to name a few.

Something to put into consideration is the fact that only you have the ability to define who you are. Also it is through the efforts that you take that you'll be able to realize your objectives and goals in life. The challenges in life are generally not bound by differences in age, and you will from time to time experience both good and bad times. The more genuine you are with yourself the more established you will be in life. The more opportunities you open yourself up to in life the more you'll be able to create a meaningful life for yourself.

As a woman you should not spend your entire lifetime worrying about your age because it is something that is natural and quite an inevitable occurrence, you will just have to grow older with time. What you need to do is to take into consideration the life you are living, to simplify this statement, you need to make every moment of your precious life count. When you understand your vision, your choices and resolutions will contribute to the fulfillment of your goals. All the best opportunities in life are bound by time and chance and not the efforts that you put in life. Also keep in mind that a heroine is not someone who is able to evade challenges but rather the one who is able to overcome them.

Chapter # 1: Principles of a Successful Woman

The principles many individuals, especially women, adhere to in life are mainly influenced by family expectations and cultural beliefs, and the main reason why many women are unhappy and muddled in life is because they took to paths that do not match their interests, passions, or skills. Everyone has her own definition of a flourishing life and this is always determined by how one perceives life. For those ladies who define success by the quantity of material possession they have, they are ultimately destined to set themselves up for failure. This is because, success, is not only associated with materialistic possessions, it is far much more than that. Success covers all aspects of your life and that is usually why it is considered very valuable.

As a female, when you strive to create the life you want, you should search for more than happiness and riches. Despite your age, you should always have your own definition of success because if you cannot clearly define what success means to you, then you might end up chasing another person's definition of it. Keep in mind that real success includes all aspects of life, be it mental state, social state, spiritual state, physical state, emotional state, and financial state.

At the same time, it is appropriate to mention that it is always easy to create a good life when you establish yourself from a state of happiness. This way you are happy with what you are doing and also in contentment with the reasons for your actions. Individual success usually occurs in so many different forms. this is because every person's concept about it is quite different. Ultimately, when you work out your own definition of success and set up your goals the right way, then you'll easily achieve your accomplishments. Everything you put your effort into in order to achieve it, life will always give you a sense of personal accomplishment once you have actually achieved it.

Chapter # 2: Techniques for crafting a better life

It's never too late when it comes to changing certain aspects in your life, especially those that are pulling you back. Another thing to put into consideration; disregarding age or vigor, there is always a part of you that yearns to be revitalized; this is where you should put most of your focus. If you seek to accomplish certain goals in your life, then you need to start making some relevant changes right away. Do not live a life where your actions are usually as a result of constrains that you experience, rather you ought to live a life where you do things because you have the freedom to do them. In life, the things that we do are only done best when we do them with willingness. No matter how different you define a prosperous life, this guide offers you simple procedures, strategies and techniques that you may apply in order for you to easily and effectively achieve your ideal lifestyle.

Establish your objectives

Goal setting is a very important feature to embrace in order to start achieving long term success. The whole idea behind this aspect, especially as a woman, is that you cannot be determined to get to a certain level or state in your life unless you define clearly what it is that you really want. Setting objectives is always very essential; you will be able to maintain your focus, it'll also allow you to invest your time appropriately and manage your resources efficiently. This is the best way to actually boost you morale.

As a woman, goal setting should come first among your agendas; this will direct your path towards success, it will remove you from your bubble and set your objectives into motion. Be the woman who lays down all her planned achievements; this will augment your short term motivation & long term vision. A woman, who sets sharp and clearly defined goals, will always feel accomplished upon the achievement of those goals. Regardless of whether your goals will realistically take a long period to actualize, setting goals is still very critical for the whole process to flow smoothly.

Conquering your fears

 As a woman, being able to overcome your fears is a skill that you need to possess; and it's quite learnable by anyone really. Many women are experiencing stagnation in their state of affairs because they usually tend to cling on to certain phobias and anxieties until it becomes a part of them. You've always got to be ready to face your fears. Whenever you are able to overcome your fears, you give yourself an opportunity to grow as an individual and you will also expand the prospects surrounding you. There are always those occasions when you have an idea that you would want to pursue or venture into, however, existence of fear may paralyze progression and prevent you from progressing with your plan. What if you decide to do something different? Inhibiting fear and its effect is not an easy fete but do not be fooled in to believing and accepting that it is not possible. Supposing you are that woman who always like to play it safe; deciding to let go of your fears is like accepting the option of being miserable if all doesn't work out over the option of constantly sheltering yourself within the confinements of your comfort zone. Take the risk and see where it leads you! The fear that you should only have is for your Creator alone.

Believing in yourself and your abilities

A common problem with so many people, not only women, is that they tend to doubt themselves and this is what usually deters them from getting to that level in life where they want to be. Never, at any moment, doubt your abilities, skills, talents, or opinions etc. The reasoning behind all this is because if you don't believe in yourself, who will? When you embrace that demeaning way of thinking, chances are you will always lock yourself out the best chances that life has in store for you.

In addition, if you want to develop and advance all aspects of your life you have to start seeing yourself the way you want others to see you; do not let the mental inferiority complex restrain you from advancing from where you currently are. It is very essential that you always believe in yourself no matter how terrible things might be. It is only through believing in yourself that you will actually develop confidence and self esteem that is vital if you want to build a better life.

If you really want to improve yourself, then it's really useful to have faith in yourself and your abilities. Do not be the kind of woman who relies on affirmations from other people in order to feel at ease on her decisions. There are so many people who look up to you, even though you might not know this, especially if you are married to someone and you have kids. Your kids have to see their mom assuming the role of a strong woman in order for them to adapt the same character; certainly something that can be deemed as is a life philosophy that will help them progress throughout life.

Operating through demanding times with tranquility
As truism as it may seem, hard work usually pays off. Whatever you want to achieve in life; you have to work towards that goal. You don't get the life you want by just sitting around, for true success; you need vigor, both of the mind and body, in order for you to attain your fullest potential. No matter how your ambitions turn out, having worked hard is a satisfying feeling in itself.

Chapter #3: Road To Self Discovery

As a woman, when your comfort zone has become a confinement, then it is time to reflect on your life; this way you can discover what you want. If you are not happy with your life then there obviously is a disconnection with your inner peace and an imminent intimate search is essential. The benefits of discovering yourself are numerous; most importantly it gives you vision and a sense of purpose. You could be busy with family life or work; you might also be filled with distractive thoughts in your mind, making it hard for you to focus on the important aspects in your life. Living is all about your present life and being able to make a difference whenever you have the chance. Everyone wants to be defined with something and the way you set your priorities should always be considered foremost. This is because; these priorities will define your future. When you don't understand yourself, you will be always allow your decisions and emotions to be dictated by external circumstances; this in turn proves that you lack goals, core beliefs, and inner values. With this kind of lifestyle, there will always be occasions when people cannot count on you for support since you are not sure whether you can count on yourself, or you cannot support yourself.

Listed below are some of the things that you might do in order to change your perspective whenever you face challenges in life;

- Identifying what you love

- Identify what brings you joy

- Writing a journal

- Talking to friends and family

- Talking to a counselor

- Meditation and Prayer

Concepts of Visualization, Imagination, and Health

The force represented by these concepts has been an awesome instrument in transforming people's dreams into reality in so many fields. Your ability as a woman to replay the vision in your conciseness of where or who you want to be in the future is key to transforming your ambition into reality. As a lady with aspiration, you likewise have the opportunity to apply these concepts in order to actually achieve your goals. Visualization for instance is an activity that involves the awakening of mental usefulness which in turn will propel you towards your dreams. Furthermore, it will also prepare you for the achievement that you are anticipating.

There is absolutely no enchantment that comes with the utilization of these concepts in order to manifest your dreams as they are just common laws. Like we had discussed earlier, all the things that you draw into your life, the universe will give back to you; and this is the reason behind why you need to constantly embrace & practice these concepts in addition to positive thinking. As a human, you are the one who is in charge of molding your own destiny; this means that you'll have to exercise the power that is hidden in your mind. Start to live your fantasy today and tomorrow it will be a reality. There are those ladies who utilize their force of perception either deliberately or unknowingly and have accomplished so much in the process.

Your intuitive personality will dependably acknowledge your rehashed musings and when it does it resets your general mindset, your propensities, and actions. This ensures that all your state of affairs is adjusted towards your objectives. The fact of the matter is that musings for the most part do not materialize each and every idea that you may have but rather those that are will defined, centered, and regularly thought of. Any vision that is engaged and loaded with enthusiastic vitality always has enough energy to interact with the universe which in turn will get things going.

Envisioning your dreams usually quickens the progress to accomplishment. What perception does is that it programs your psyche, actuates your innovative subconscious, initiates the law of attraction, and it additionally helps you to build your interior inspiration. What you concentrate on, you will eventually draw in and this is so in light of the fact that your thoughts dependably attempt to express themselves in your life.

You ought to likewise realize that perception is really a mainstream technique that is utilized by various prosperous individuals from all kinds of different backgrounds. These include individuals like Facebook's

Zuckenberg, Oprah, and Bill Gates, just to name a few; they all applied the power of visualization to propel their visions into reality. You are therefore urged to make perception a habit. The most essential variable in perception that you have to put as a primary concern is the significance of being able to comprehend your desires in the first place. It is quite simple for your brain to concentrate on something that it has a more profound comprehension of and because of this; you ought to guarantee yourself that every one of your objectives and dreams are set in your psyche.

Chapter #4: Visualization

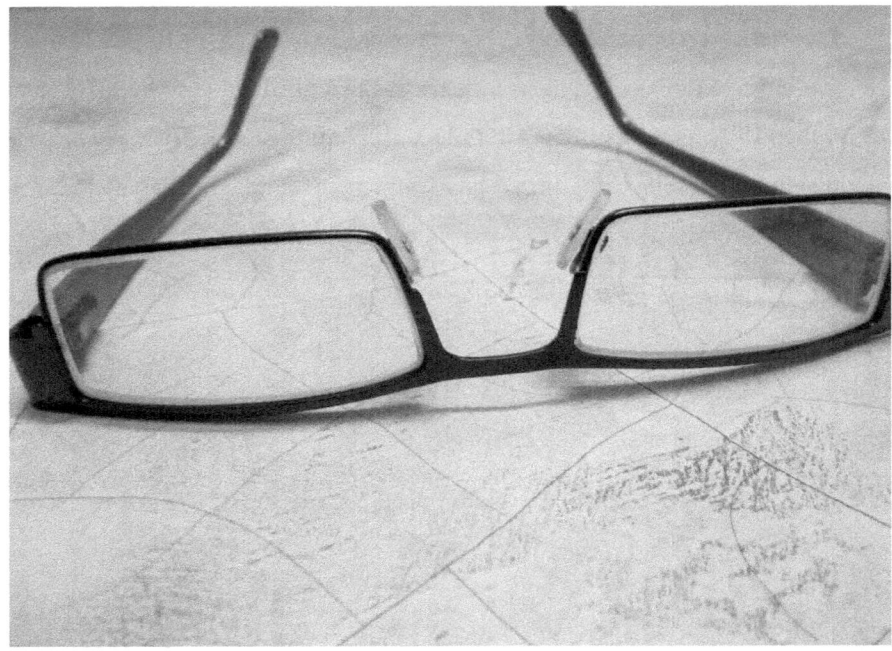

It is quite easy to visualize, however, there are some key points that you'll need to learn in order to effectively fast-track your results. Please note that visualization can be applied in all aspects of life; and it will truly set you in the right mood. In addition, it will put you in a suitable position to accomplish all that you want in life. Listed below are the most important steps that you need to follow for a proper visualization procedure:

Clarify your goals

It'll be difficult to achieve something if you are not aware of how to go about your venture, your first step should always be to set some goals. The goals that you have in mind should also be specific, achievable, and also comprehensive. Setting realistic goals is a very important point of focus; in order to nail this, you'll have to start out small and progress each step at a time. Before you can begin believing in a goal you must have an idea of what the outcome of achieving it will feel like. Jot down your visualization goals; this will give you a specific structure to follow and also a fall back plan in case there is any setbacks.

Stage management strategies

After you have defined the actions that you are going to take in order to achieve your goals, write down in a comprehensive manner, all the effective actions that you are going to take to attain your goal. Before you start the visualization exercise, master all these steps so that it will be easier for you to visualize yourself doing these actions.

Set an appropriate time-span

Unless you set aside some time for visualization, it will very difficult for you to commit to the process. Setting aside time will also determine the appropriate time of the day when to do the actual visualization. You can decide to visualize early in the morning or just before you go to sleep. It is also imperative that you visualize every time before you attend any event and especially before taking any action towards the achievement of your goal.

Set the appropriate mood

For effective visualization, you have to set the right mood for it to be successful; it is of the essence that you be prepared physically, mentally, and emotionally. You can achieve this state by first, being in the right environment for the process; a quiet and comfortable place is preferable. Find a comfortable body posture, take in a few deep breaths and create some room in your mind for visualization.

Start with the end goal

Any time you want to visualize, it is very important that you begin the process by picturing your ultimate goal. This is where you start by living the dream virtually in your mind. Picture that goal and try to envision what it feels like to have achieved your dream. Try to make the vision as detailed as possible in order to make it more realistic.

Visualize your actions

Once you are virtually at that point when you are living your vision, begin rehearsing your courses of action. If your actions are many, then you can begin to break them down with regard to the specific goals. And while you are doing all these things, ensure that you able to generate the emotions & feelings that you intend to have once you have accomplished your goal.

Chapter # 5: Meditation

Meditation is a practice where one focuses on her breathing and rids her mind of any depressing thoughts; a pure relaxation technique. With the current hectic and demanding lifestyle that we face each day, one always feels the pressure and at times it can be quite challenging to handle. These kinds of sensations can really bring about unhappiness, frustrations, and impatience and it can get to the extent where your health begins to deteriorate. At first, you might think that you have no time to meditate but what you need to know is that this practice will improve your time management skills because it'll make you calm and focused. Meditation helps you have inner peace by putting you in a position where you are able to understand yourself and your life in general. It also gives you a chance for you to turn any situation that you might be facing from a negative one to a positive one. Through meditation you'll be able to transform from an unhappy lady to someone who's happy and also from disturbed person to one who is peaceful. The inspiration behind practicing meditation is that it will help you free your mind of any negative thoughts and maintain your focus on present matters at hand.

Benefits of Meditation

- Increases blood flow in the body and slows the heart rate.
- It reduces the activity of harmful viruses and emotional distress.
- It helps with weight loss.
- It relaxes the nervous system.
- It improves the body's immune system.
- Enhances energy, strength and vigor.
- Slows down the process of aging.
- It prevents, slows or controls the pain of chronic diseases.

- Cures headaches and migraines.
- It assists with focus and concentration.
- Improves learning ability and memory.
- It improves creativity through expansive thinking.
- It improves a person's social behavior.
- It enhances the capacity of intimate contact with the loved ones.
- Purification of one's character and development of the will power.
- It develops harmony in the mind, body & spirit.
- It helps one to get a better perception about their lives.
- It helps develop a deeper relationship and understanding with God.
- It reduces feelings of loneliness.
- It improves ones mood and also the psychological well-being.
- Increases mental strength, resilience and also emotional intelligence.
- It boosts self-esteem and self-acceptance.

Learning Meditation

Meditation does not require you to make drastic changes in your life, all that you need are some minutes, and the following context offers some tips on how to start the process;

a)   View it as a simple relaxation technique:

Meditation simply offers an opportunity where you can relax and embark into deeper concentration. Thoughts that will relieve you of stress by getting into that zone where you have peace of mind. This can be simply achieved by choosing a suitable environment that is free from disturbance. Sit down and close your eyes; take a deep breath and just relax.

b)   Choose a conducive style of meditation:

Closing your eyes slowly, direct your soft unfocused gaze downwards; take a few deep breaths through intentional relaxation of your body. This is achieved by tensing and relaxing your body muscles. If you are a visual person, try and focus on a certain image that will eventually lead you to achieve that intimate association with yourself, that's the primary goal. As you begin to develop an improved focus & energy, the more it will become easy for you to achieve total concentration.

c)   Schedule a practice session:

You need to schedule a meditation session depending on how you see fit, how much you feel the need of it. A session a day would be quite convenient. The process should be done regularly and consistently. You need to commit yourself to the practice in order for you to be able to make the most out of the entire process.

d)   Do not resist your thoughts:

It is normal during a meditation session (especially for beginners) for the brain to wonder into the deepest thoughts, though some might be disturbing, it is part of the whole process. Do not resist the brain to work on its expansive exploration nature, it will gradually venture into more peaceful thoughts; this is the key to positive meditation.

e)   Rearrange your thoughts:

During the session, negative thoughts may cloud the mind, especially at the beginning when one is trying to focus. You can reprogram your thoughts by using certain positive phrases that you may have learnt from religious books, songs, and so on. You can try to repeat these phrases anytime you have negative thoughts blocking your focus; an alternative way would be to think about the good moments that you had in your life; this will assist to channel the brain away from the negative thoughts.

Schedule a challenge
This is the part where you need to challenge yourself to have meditation session consistently for a period of not less than 10 days consecutively without failure. This way you'll be able to learn how to focus your mind until meditation becomes like a normal practice to you.

The Process of Concentration Meditation
Unlike the normal meditation, this type of meditation technique normally involves focusing on a specific point for concentration. It can be very challenging to achieve concentration but it is certainly not impossible. If you

are learning this technique for the first time, you can try practicing it for a few minutes and then gradually improving on the time. Eventually with time you will improve. The objective of this technique of meditation is so that you can enhance your attention to sound, images, your breath, or any other form of energy within your surroundings. This usually helps the mind to be more calm, stable, relaxed, and grounded. As a learner, try focusing on your breath in the meditation sessions as this will be easier for you to master.

Process of Concentration Meditation

1. Find a comfortable sitting or standing posture. You can decide to sit with your legs crossed but not on top of each other; try alternating your legs to find the most comfortable position.

2. If you want to do your meditation in a sitting position, put your palms on your laps or the knees and if it's a standing posture, let your arms fall at your side.

3. Next step, ensure that you are completely relaxed.

4. Start by breathing naturally but the breaths that you take in should gradually become deeper than the norm.

5. Start monitoring your inhaling and exhaling exercises while maintaining them deep.

6. Clear your thoughts; do this by accepting any thought that enters your mind. Maintain your breathing while you are at it.

7. Do this until you achieve the feeling you want but also keep in mind not to make it too long.

Chapter # 6: How to maintain a healthy lifestyle

As a woman, with time you are bound to experience certain body changes. This is usually due to a number of reasons; it doesn't have to be a negative factor that hinders you from getting what you want in life, especially if you decide to live a healthy lifestyle. This transition that all women experience is actually a natural process; mostly because of the process of maturity. You need to understand that healthy living and feeling great about your choices is something that you should strive to attain. It is not hard to achieve this because all you need to do is to practice healthy living habits; this will maintain you at a healthy aging gap where you will be constantly reinventing yourself. You are therefore encouraged to find new interests, be connected to their loved ones, learn to adapt to changes and also you need to stay physically and socially active. To maintain a proper & healthy lifestyle, you should try your best to exercise the following strategies:

1. Eat a healthy diet and also reduce your calorie consumption.

2. Exercise or do any kind of physical activity a part of your daily routine.

3. Maintain a habit of socializing and having fun.

4. Do activities that keep you mentally active.

5. Avoid smoking and drinking, and too much alcohol.

6. Go for regular health checkups.

7. Reduce your stress levels using the information provided earlier in the guide.

8.   Maintain healthy sleeping habits.

9. You will also be able to realize that your body needs more attention by observing the following signs:

10. Increase or decrease of body weight.

11. Poor concentration.

12. Change in sleeping habit.

13. Continuous fatigue.

14. Constant feeling of depression.

15. Increased irritability.

16. Change in eating habits.

17. Pale skin.

18. Unusual Body aches and pains.

19. Increased level of confusion.

20. Interminable feeling of sadness.

Conclusion

It is my hope that this guide was able to help you as a woman to understand all that it takes to get what you want, how to achieve a complete lifestyle transformation, and improving your health and general well being. It has covered so much of what you need to know and you are sure of having an idea about how and where you should start from in order for you to start living your dreams.

Our time on this earth is realistically limited and so it very important for you to make good use of the available time by embracing every single moment with positivity. We all age with time, the same way we experience some changes in our bodies. As a woman you may find it hard to accept and adapt and this is why this eBook is vital for similar occurrences in women's' life. Nonetheless, it is very important that you learn to make the best out of life.

So much aspects have been covered, all of which aim to enhance specific areas of your life and it is actually an opportunity for you to utilize the content of this guide to its full potential; ultimately you will realize that all the effort that you put into reading this book will be worth your precious time.

About the Author

Dr. Usman is an MD, now pursuing his post-graduation degree. As a medical doctor, he has deep insight in all aspects of health, fitness and nutrition.

He is a certified nutritionist and a personal trainer. With these qualifications, he has helped countless people reach their health, fitness and weight loss goals.

Dr. Usman is an avid researcher with 20+ publications in internationally accepted peer reviewed journals.

He is an accomplished writer with more than 5 years of writing experience. In this time, he has produced countless blogs, articles and research work on topics related to health, fitness and nutrition.

He is a published author with more than 100+ books published and several more in the pipe line.

Finally, he runs his own blog and posts health, fitness and nutrition related articles there regularly. You can visit his blog at http://hcures.com/

Check out some of the other JD-Biz Publishing books
Gardening Series on Amazon

Health Learning Series

THE MAGIC OF **GOOSEBERRIES** FOR HEALTH AND BEAUTY — Natural Remedy Series

THE MAGIC OF **YOGURT** FOR COOKING AND BEAUTY — Natural Remedy Series

THE MAGIC OF **LEMONS** USING LEMONS FOR HEALTH AND BEAUTY — Natural Remedy Series

THE MAGIC OF **CHILLIES** FOR COOKING AND HEALING — Natural Remedy Series

THE MAGIC OF **ONIONS** ONIONS IN CUISINE TO CURE AND TO HEAL — Natural Remedy Series

THE MAGIC OF **RADISHES** TO CURE AND TO HEAL — Natural Remedy Series

THE MAGIC OF **CARROTS** TO CURE AND TO HEAL — Natural Remedy Series

THE HEALTH BENEFITS OF **OREGANO** FOR COOKING AND HEALTH — Natural Remedy Series

The Magic Of **MARIGOLDS** Marigolds for Health And Beauty — Natural Remedy Series

THE HEALTH BENEFITS OF **CINNAMON** — Natural Remedy Series

THE MAGIC OF **COCONUTS** FOR COOKING & HEALTH — Health Learning Series

THE MAGIC OF **CLOVES** FOR HEALING AND COOKING — Health Learning Series

THE MAGIC OF **ASAFETIDA** FOR COOKING AND HEALING — Health Learning Series

THE MAGIC OF **NEEM** MARGOSA TO HEAL — Natural Remedy Series

THE MAGIC OF **SALT** TO HEAL AND FOR BEAUTY — Natural Remedy Series

THE MAGIC OF **POMEGRANATES** FOR HEALTH AND BEAUTY — Natural Remedy Series

THE MAGIC OF **DRY FRUIT AND SPICES** REMEDIES AND RECIPES — Natural Remedy Series

THE HEALTH BENEFITS OF **TURMERIC CURCUMIN** FOR COOKING AND HEALTH — Natural Remedy Series

THE MAGIC OF **ALOE VERA** — Natural Remedy Series

THE MAGIC OF **VEGETABLES** ANCIENT HEALING REMEDIES AND TIPS — Natural Remedy Series

THE HEALTH BENEFITS OF **ROSEMARY** FOR COOKING AND HEALTH — Natural Remedy Series

THE MAGIC OF **PEPPER & PEPPERCORNS** FOR COOKING & HEALING — Natural Remedy Series

THE MAGIC OF **MILK, BUTTER AND CHEESE** FOR COOKING & HEALING — Natural Remedy Series

THE MAGIC OF **CARDAMOMS** FOR COOKING AND HEALTH — Health Learning Series

THE HEALTH BENEFITS OF **BLACK CUMIN** FOR COOKING AND HEALTH — Natural Remedy Series

THE MAGIC OF **BASIL-TULSI** TO HEAL NATURALLY — Health Learning Series

THE MAGIC OF **SPICES** FOR HEALTH AND CUISINE — Natural Remedy Series

THE MAGIC OF **ROSES** FOR COOKING AND BEAUTY — Natural Remedy Series

The Miraculous Healing Powers of **GINGER** — Natural Remedy Series

The Miracle of **HONEY** — Natural Remedy Series

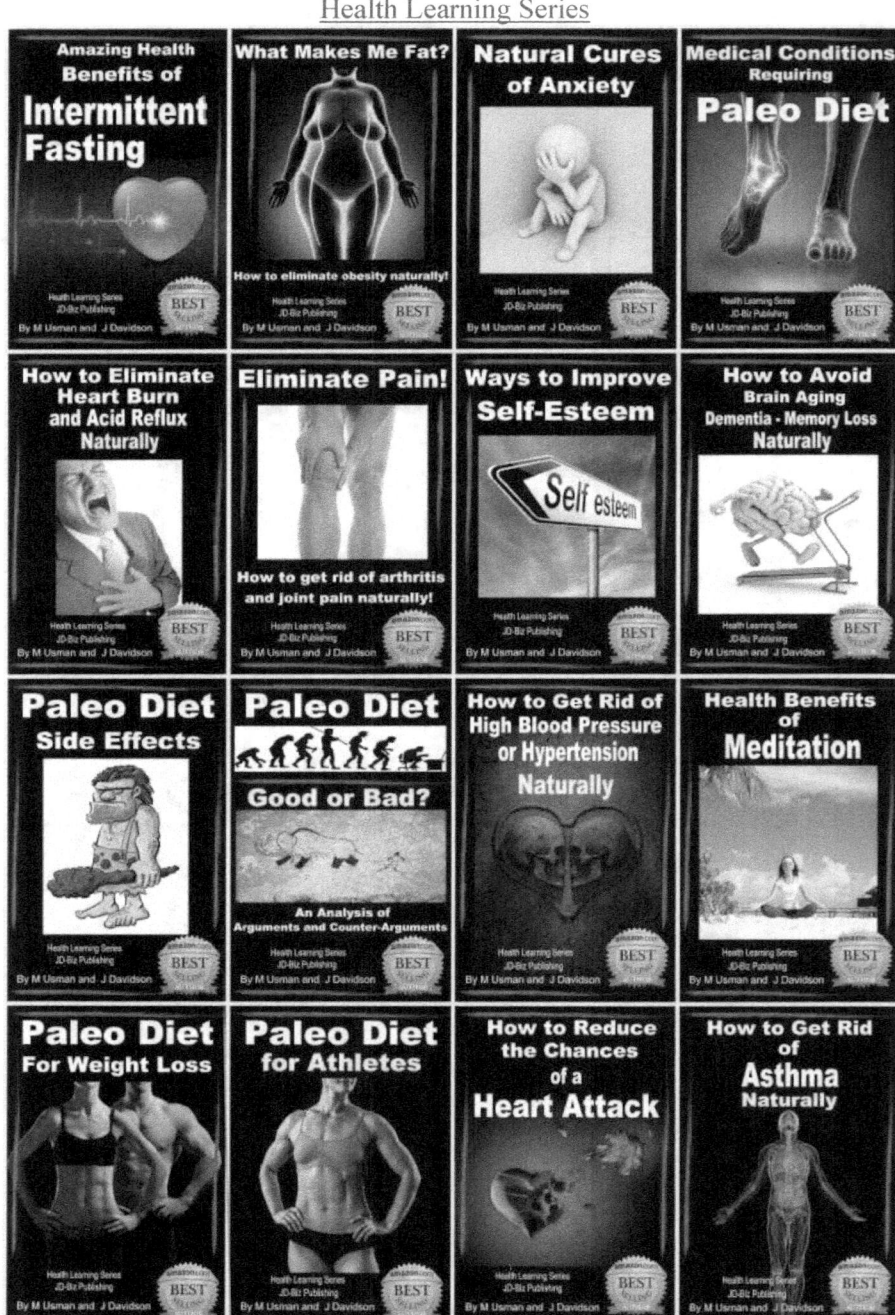

Amazing Animal Book Series

Learn To Draw Series

How to Build and Plan Books

Entrepreneur Book Series

Our books are available at

1. Amazon.com

2. Barnes and Noble

3. Itunes

4. Kobo

5. Smashwords

6. Google Play Books

Download Free Books!
http://MendonCottageBooks.com

Publisher

JD-Biz Corp

P O Box 374

Mendon, Utah 84325

http://www.jd-biz.com/